Illinois

by Terri Sievert

Consultant:
Thomas F. Schwartz
Illinois State Historian
Illinois Historic Preservation Agency

Capstone press
Mankato, Minnesota

Capstone Press
151 Good Counsel Drive • P.O. Box 669 • Mankato, Minnesota 56002
http://www.capstone-press.com

Library of Congress Cataloging-in-Publication Data
Sievert, Terri.
    Illinois / by Terri Sievert.
    v. cm.—(Land of liberty)
    Contents: About Illinois—Land, climate, and wildlife—History of Illinois—
Government and politics—Economy and resources—People and culture.
    Includes bibliographical references (p. 61) and index.
    ISBN 0-7368-1581-3 (hardcover)
    1. Illinois—Juvenile literature. [1. Illinois.] I. Title. II. Series.
F541.3 .S54 2003
977.3—dc21   2002012476

Summary: An introduction to the geography, history, government, politics,
economy, resources, people, and culture of Illinois, including maps, charts,
and a recipe.

Editorial Credits
Megan Schoeneberger, editor; Jennifer Schonborn, series designer; Linda Clavel,
    book designer; Angi Gahler, illustrator; Deirdre Barton, photo researcher;
    Eric Kudalis, product planning editor

Photo Credits
Cover images: Grant Park in Chicago, Illinois, Victor Englebert; railroad tracks
    in Stelle, Illinois, Panoramic Images/Mark Segal

Capstone Press/Gary Sundermeyer, 54; Corbis, 18; Corbis/Bettmann, 21, 32–33;
Corbis/Bill Ross, 44–45; Corbis/David Muench, 8; Corbis/Richard A. Cooke, 4;
Corbis/Richard Hamilton Smith, 16, 38, 46; Corbis/Tom Bean, 14; Doranne
Jacobson, 26; Getty Images/Hulton Archive, 20, 31; Getty Images/Tim
Boyle/Newsmakers, 43; The Image Finders/Bruce Leighty, 15; Image Ideas,
Inc./Paul Hartley, 56; One Mile Up, Inc., 55 (both); Panoramic Images/New
Moon, 50–51; Panoramic Images/Richard Day, 12–13; PhotoDisc, Inc., 1; Stock
Montage, Inc., 22, 23, 24, 28, 29, 39, 53, 58; Stock Montage, Inc./Tom Neiman,
63; UNICORN Stock Photos/Joel Dexter, 34, 40; USFWS/Hollingsworth, John
and Karen, 57; U.S. Postal Service, 59

Artistic Effects
Corbis, Digital Stock, PhotoDisc, Inc.

1 2 3 4 5 6 08 07 06 05 04 03

Table of Contents

At the Cahokia Mounds, visitors climb to the top of Monks Mound to imagine how the ancient city looked.

Chapter 1

About Illinois

In southern Illinois, visitors can climb 100 feet (30 meters) to the top of Monks Mound. The mound is the largest of hundreds of land formations called the Cahokia Mounds. Some of the mounds have rounded tops, while others are flat.

From about A.D. 900 to 1500, a group of about 15,000 people called the Mound Builders built the mounds in their city. Some of the mounds contain graves. Larger mounds like Monks Mound probably were platforms for their leaders' homes. From the top of the high mounds, the leaders could look down and see the entire city.

By 1500, the city was empty. Archaeologists do not know why the Mound Builders left. Perhaps the land flooded, or the

> *"We have seen nothing like this river that we enter, as regards its fertility of soil, its prairies and woods."*
>
> —Father Jacques Marquette, one of the first Europeans to travel to Illinois, in 1673

people may have run out of food and firewood. Today, visitors climb the steps of Monks Mound and imagine what the city was like.

The Prairie State

Illinois is in the Midwest. Three rivers border this state. The Ohio River to the south separates Illinois and Kentucky. The Wabash River makes up part of the state's eastern border with Indiana. The Mississippi River forms the western border of Illinois. It divides the state from Iowa and Missouri. Wisconsin is north of Illinois. Lake Michigan touches the northeast corner of Illinois.

More than 12 million people live in Illinois. That number makes Illinois the fifth most populated state. Most of the people in Illinois live in Chicago and other large cities. Others live in smaller cities and on farms on the wide prairies. The prairies have given the state its nickname, the Prairie State.

Illinois' Cities

Legend
- ★ Capital
- ● City
- ～ River

WISCONSIN

IOWA

MISSOURI

INDIANA

KENTUCKY

ILLINOIS

Lake Michigan

● Rockford

Chicago ●

● Joliet

● Moline

● Peoria

● Bloomington

Springfield ✪

● Decatur

● Vandalia

Mississippi River

Wabash River

Ohio River

N
W E
S

Scale
Miles
0   20   40   60   80
0 20 40 60 80 100
Kilometers

Many interesting rock formations can be found in the Shawnee National Forest.

Chapter 2

Land, Climate, and Wildlife

Three main land regions cover Illinois. The Shawnee Hills and Gulf Coastal Plain are smaller regions. They are in the southern tip of the state. The broad, flat land of the Central Plains makes up the largest region. This region covers 90 percent of the state.

Hills and Rivers

The Shawnee Hills is a narrow region in southern Illinois. Trees cover the hilly land. The hills connect to the Ozark Mountains in Missouri. Some people call the Shawnee Hills the "Illinois Ozarks." The Shawnee Hills are about 70 miles

(115 kilometers) long. The width of the hills varies between 5 and 40 miles (8 and 64 kilometers). The Shawnee National Forest covers a large part of this area. It has rock formations such as Camel Rock and Fat Man's Squeeze.

The Gulf Coastal Plain region is at the state's southern edge. The Mississippi River forms the western border of this area. The Ohio River lies to the east. Early settlers called the land between the two rivers "Egypt." They thought it looked like the fertile land near the Nile River in Egypt. This region contains the state's lowest point. Along the Mississippi River, the land is 279 feet (85 meters) above sea level.

The Central Plains

Moving sheets of ice called glaciers once flattened most of the Central Plains in northern and central Illinois. They carried rocks and trees across the land. The glaciers left rich soil.

The Central Plains has three sections. In central Illinois, the soil of the Till Plains is good for farming. This area is part of the corn belt that includes Ohio, Kansas, and Nebraska. In the corn belt, a great deal of the land is used to grow corn.

The Great Lakes Plains region surrounds Chicago. This area is mostly flat, but it has some small hills. Before the city was built, the land was a low, wet swamp.

Illinois' Land Features

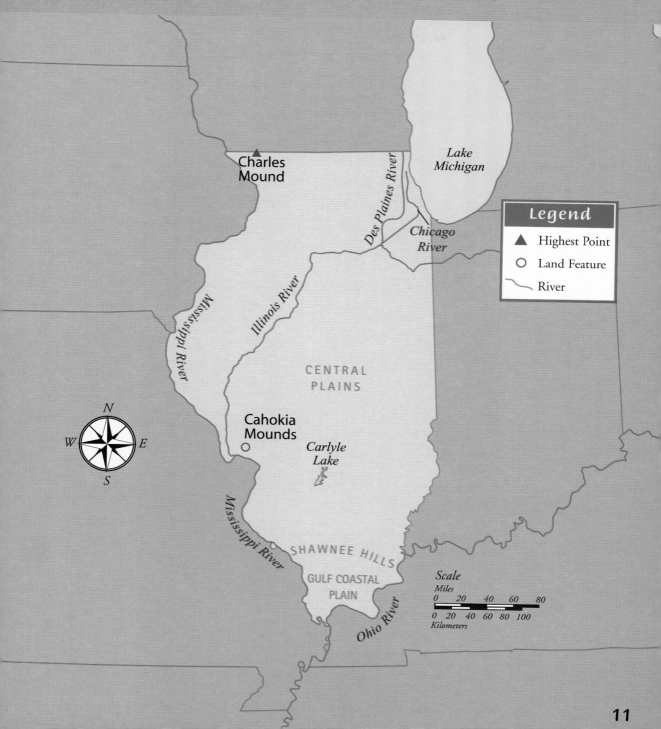

Charles
Mound ▲

*Lake
Michigan*

Des Plaines River

*Chicago
River*

Legend
▲ Highest Point
○ Land Feature
〜 River

Mississippi River

Illinois River

CENTRAL
PLAINS

Cahokia
Mounds ○

*Carlyle
Lake*

N
W   E
S

Mississippi River

SHAWNEE HILLS

GULF COASTAL
PLAIN

Ohio River

Scale
Miles
0   20   40   60   80

0 20 40 60 80 100
Kilometers

The Driftless Area is in northwestern Illinois. Glaciers did not cover the Driftless Area. This region has high hills and deep valleys. Near the region's northwestern corner, the state's highest point, Charles Mound, rises 1,235 feet (376 meters).

Climate

Weather in Illinois changes quickly. Winds blowing across the flat land bring cool air from the north or warm air from the south. Severe weather results when cool and warm air meet. The wind may bring blizzards, thunderstorms, and tornadoes.

Tornadoes have killed more people in Illinois than in any other state. In 1925, a tornado killed 606 people in southern Illinois.

The weather in northern Illinois is slightly cooler than the weather in southern Illinois. In January, the average temperature in the north is 25 degrees Fahrenheit (minus 4 degrees Celsius). In southern Illinois, the average January temperature is 36 degrees Fahrenheit (2 degrees Celsius).

The southern part of the state usually gets more precipitation than the north. The south gets about

Winds blow across Illinois' flat land, causing weather to change quickly.

Big Bluestem

Big bluestem is the tallest prairie grass in Illinois. It grows 8 to 10 feet (2 to 3 meters) tall. The grass is green in summer. In autumn, it turns blue-purple. It usually grows in wet soil and lowlands. But its deep roots help it survive when rainfall is light.

Big bluestem also is called "turkey feet" or "turkey claw." Its seeds grow on spikes that look like a turkey's foot. In 1989, the Illinois government made big bluestem the state prairie grass of Illinois.

40 inches (102 centimeters) of precipitation each year. The north receives about 34 inches (86 centimeters) of precipitation.

Rivers and Lakes

About 500 rivers and streams flow through Illinois. The largest river entirely in Illinois is the Illinois River. It is 273 miles (439 kilometers) long. It flows across the center of the state before emptying into the Mississippi River. The

Illinois River is linked by canals to the Des Plaines and Chicago Rivers. These rivers and canals connect Lake Michigan to the Mississippi River. This link allows ships to reach the Atlantic Ocean from the Mississippi River.

Illinois has few lakes. Lake Michigan has 63 miles (101 kilometers) of shoreline in Illinois. Carlyle Lake, the

People in Chicago can drive along the shore of Lake Michigan. The lake is the sixth largest freshwater lake in the world.

largest lake in Illinois, covers 24,580 acres (9,948 hectares). Crab Orchard Lake is in the southern part of the state. Up to 120,000 Canadian geese spend winters near this large lake.

Wildlife

Illinois' swamps, lakes, and prairies offer homes for many kinds of animals. Great blue herons nest along Illinois' rivers. Pheasants and quail hide in the tall grass of the plains. Snapping turtles and painted turtles sun themselves on rocks in streams.

As cities and farms replace prairies, some animals and birds such as the prairie chicken are in danger of dying out.

Many types of fish swim in the lakes, streams, and rivers of Illinois. The bluegill is the state fish. Perch, pike, and sunfish also are common.

Endangered Animals

Some animals in Illinois struggle to survive as the prairies slowly disappear. People have built cities and farms on prairie land. In 1820, Illinois had 22 million acres (9 million hectares) of prairie. Less than 1 percent of that prairie land remains. The upland sandpiper once had plenty of room in the Illinois prairie. This brown bird now nests wherever grassland can be found. Other animals in danger are the Indiana bat, the spotted turtle, and the prairie chicken.

The state plans to replant some prairies for animal habitat. With its Open Land Trust program, the state buys land to preserve open areas. By 2002, the Open Land Trust had added 16,320 acres (9,111 hectares) to Pyramid State Park in southern Illinois. It also established nature preserves in Chicago and the surrounding cities.

The Kaskaskia Indians were among the five major tribes in the Illinois Confederacy. This illustration shows a Kaskaskia Indian in traditional clothing.

Chapter 3

History of Illinois

Before French settlers arrived, groups of American Indians lived on the Illinois prairie. The Illini or Illiniwek were among the first groups to live in Illinois. Their name meant "The Men" or "The People." They also are known as the Illinois Confederacy. The five major tribes in this group were the Cahokia, Kaskaskia, Michigamea, Peoria, and Tamaroa tribes.

The French and the British

The French were the first Europeans to explore the Illinois prairie. In 1673, a governor in present-day Canada sent two men to find the Mississippi River. These two men, Louis

Father Jacques Marquette (standing, wearing black robe) founded a mission to teach the Illinois Indians about Christianity.

Jolliet and Father Jacques Marquette, traveled south along the present-day border of Illinois. Marquette founded a mission at a Kaskaskia Indian village in 1675.

Illinois became part of the French colony of Louisiana in 1717. But the British wanted to control all land west of their colonies. The British and French fought over this land during the French and Indian wars. After the British won the wars in 1763, the Illinois region came under British control.

During the Revolutionary War (1775–1783), the British sent few troops to Illinois. This fact helped American Lieutenant Colonel George Rogers Clark from Virginia. He led 175 men called the Big Knives. On July 4, 1778, they surprised British soldiers and captured the town of Kaskaskia.

After the capture of Kaskaskia, Illinois became a county of Virginia because Virginia's governor had supported Clark. In 1784, Maryland asked other states to give up claims in

George Rogers Clark organized a group of men who captured the town of Kaskaskia from the British during the Revolutionary War.

western lands. Virginia and other states agreed and gave Illinois to the national government. In turn, Maryland joined the rest of the colonies in signing the Articles of Confederation. This document formed the first federal government in the United States.

In 1787, Illinois became part of the Northwest Territory. This area also included land in present-day Ohio, Indiana,

During the Fort Dearborn Massacre, American Indians attacked settlers and soldiers as they tried to leave the fort. The Indians were angry because white settlers had taken much of their land.

Chicago Is Born

In 1779, a Haitian man named Jean Baptiste Point du Sable built a trading post on the Chicago River. His business did well. When he moved to Missouri in 1800, he left behind a permanent settlement. This city eventually became Chicago.

Michigan, Wisconsin, and part of Minnesota. In 1800, the U.S. government divided the Northwest Territory because more people had settled there. Illinois became part of the Indiana Territory.

Illinois Territory

The U.S. government formed the Illinois Territory in 1809. It included parts of present-day Illinois and Wisconsin.

Settlers and American Indians often fought over land. The government built forts to protect the settlers. One of these forts was Fort Dearborn. The fort was on the shore of Lake Michigan near the settlement of Chicago.

Trouble between settlers and American Indians increased in 1812. In August 1812, the U.S. government ordered the settlers and soldiers at Fort Dearborn to move to a safer place. As the white people tried to flee, American Indian warriors attacked. About 100 settlers and soldiers were killed. The attack became known as the Fort Dearborn Massacre.

Statehood

Illinois became the 21st state on December 3, 1818. At first, the state's northern border touched just the southern tip of

Black Hawk led the Sauk and Fox Indian tribes in a fight to keep their land in Illinois.

Lake Michigan. This border left the city of Chicago in present-day Wisconsin. Nathaniel Pope, a government official, then asked to move the border north. This change gave Illinois some Lake Michigan shoreline. Chicago became part of the state of Illinois.

Early settlers' need for land forced American Indian tribes farther west. In 1831, the government ordered the Sauk and the Fox tribes to move west of the Mississippi River. In 1832, about 1,000 tribe members returned to Illinois to plant crops. A man named Black Hawk was their leader. Illinois soldiers and federal troops tried to stop the tribes. A war began, later known as the Black Hawk War. Even though Black Hawk and his people won some battles, they were forced into Wisconsin by the end of 1832.

A Transportation Center

Illinois' location between Lake Michigan and the Mississippi River made it a natural transportation center. The Illinois and Michigan Canal, finished in 1848, linked the Illinois River with Lake Michigan. It allowed ships to travel through the Great Lakes to the Mississippi River and the Gulf of Mexico.

Civil War

In 1858, Illinois politicians Abraham Lincoln and Stephen Douglas ran for the U.S. Senate. Lincoln and Douglas met in seven cities to argue about slavery. Lincoln argued against slavery.

Lincoln lost the election, but he gained national attention. He was elected president in 1860. Many states feared Lincoln

Abraham Lincoln (standing, center) and Stephen Douglas (front row, seated left of Lincoln) debated the issue of slavery during an 1858 campaign for the U.S. Senate.

would end slavery. Seven Southern states left the Union by the time Lincoln took office on March 4, 1861. Soon after, four more states left the Union. These 11 states formed the Confederate States of America. The Civil War (1861–1865) between the North and South began.

About 255,000 Union soldiers from Illinois fought during the Civil War. One soldier was Union General Ulysses S. Grant from Galena. After the war ended, he served two terms as president.

Disaster and Recovery in Chicago

The summer of 1871 was dry in Illinois. On October 8, 1871, Chicago burned. The fire began in the evening. It lasted 31 hours and burned Chicago's many wooden buildings, streets, and sidewalks. In the end, the Great Chicago Fire of 1871 destroyed about 17,000 buildings. At least 300 people died.

Chicagoans used the fire as a chance to improve their city. Builders designed new buildings with steel frames. Steel was

The Great Fire

Historians agree that the Great Chicago Fire began in the O'Leary barn. Kate O'Leary sold milk to her neighbors. At first, people thought one of Mrs. O'Leary's cows must have kicked over a lantern. The spark from the lantern could have set the hay in the barn on fire. After the fire, the people of Chicago wanted to know if this theory were true. They talked to at least 50 people, including Mrs. O'Leary. Still, they failed to find the real cause. They wrote in their report that "whether it originated [began] from a spark blown from a chimney on that windy night, or was set on fire by human agency, we are unable to determine."

stronger and lighter than stone. The first of these new buildings towered over Chicago's streets by 1885. The skyscraper was 10 stories tall.

The Early 1900s

In the late 1800s, many workers in Illinois were not happy. Factory workers earned low pay. They worked long hours in

unsafe conditions. Workers stopped working to protest poor
working conditions and low pay.

On May 4, 1886, workers met in Chicago to protest how
police handled these strikes. Police came to stop the rally.
Fighting started after someone threw a bomb into the group.
Eight people died during the event that became known as the
Haymarket Riot.

Through all the problems, Illinois continued to gain
workers. By 1900, one-half of the people of Illinois worked

Conflicts between
workers and
employees led to the
Haymarket Riot, a
fight in which eight
people died.

in cities. Europeans came to work in Illinois, as did African Americans from the South. Chicago became the second largest city in the country.

The United States entered World War I (1914–1918) in 1917. Men trained at the Great Lakes Naval Training Center in Chicago. The 33rd Division, also known as the Prairie Division, was made up of men from Illinois.

Prohibition and the Great Depression

After the war, crime increased in Illinois. In the 1920s, a law made making or selling alcohol illegal. Gangs began to sell illegal alcohol during this period, which was called Prohibition. Al Capone led one of these gangs in Chicago. On February 14, 1929, members of Capone's gang killed seven members of the Bugs Moran gang. The murders became known as the St. Valentine's Day Massacre.

Before the Great Depression (1929–1939), cities in Illinois continued to grow. Low prices of farm products had forced farmers to leave their farms. Many people wanted work in factories. After the stock market crashed in 1929, many workers lost jobs.

World War II and Post-War Years

In 1941, the United States entered World War II (1939–1945). New jobs in manufacturing helped the state's economy climb out of the Great Depression. More than 800 factories in Illinois made aircraft and aircraft parts.

The 1968 Democratic National Convention

The 1960s were tense in the nation and in Illinois. At the 1968 Democratic National Convention in Chicago, people protested the Vietnam War (1954–1975). More than 25,000 police officers and other agents tried to keep protesters away

Al Capone was a powerful gang leader during the period of Prohibition, when alcohol was illegal.

from the convention. TV cameras showed police beating protesters. The weeklong convention ended with 119 police officers and 100 protesters injured. More than 500 people were arrested.

Chicago suffered after the 1970s. People moved from the inner city to suburbs. They left run-down houses and a rising crime rate. During this time, Illinois' growth slowed.

Illinois communities have looked for new ways to make money. When an Air Force base in Rantoul closed in 1993, almost one-third of the city's population left. The city attracted new businesses. A manufacturing plant, business offices, and a museum filled the empty base. In six years, the community's population jumped from 8,000 to about 17,000.

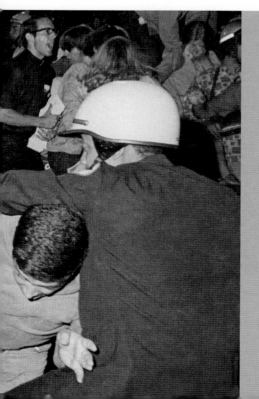

A fight between police and protesters broke out during the 1968 Democratic National Convention in Chicago.

Lawmakers meet in the Illinois capitol. This building cost $4.5 million to build over 20 years.

Chapter 4

Government and Politics

In 1818, Illinois wrote its first constitution. Voters can choose to change the state's constitution every 20 years. Lawmakers then write a new one at a state convention.

Illinois has had three capital cities. Kaskaskia was the first capital. In 1820, lawmakers moved the capital to Vandalia. They wanted to encourage more settlers to live in the central part of the state. To attract even more settlers, lawmakers moved the capital to Springfield in 1839.

Branches of Government

The state's legislature is called the General Assembly. This group includes the state senate and the state house of representatives.

"We've proven that partisans need not be enemies. It is possible to reach across the aisle and work together for the good of everyone. One by one, we've gotten things done —and this state is the better for it."
—George H. Ryan, governor of Illinois, in a speech in 2001

Senate districts are divided into three groups. Senators in each group serve a combination of two- and four-year terms. Representatives serve two-year terms. Members of the assembly make laws. Along with the governor, they prepare the state budget.

The governor leads the executive branch of government in Illinois. The governor of Illinois has many jobs. He or she must accept bills before they become laws. A governor can refuse a bill by vetoing it. The governor also can release prisoners from jail. He or she manages the state's military and calls emergency sessions of the General Assembly.

The judicial branch includes three types of courts. Voters elect judges to the Illinois Supreme Court, Appellate Court, and circuit courts. The supreme court is the top court. Seven justices serve in this court. The circuit court in Cook County is the largest court in the United States. It has more than 400 judges.

Illinois' State Government

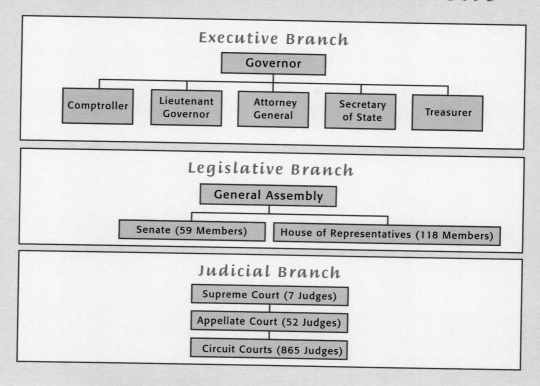

Executive Branch

Governor

- Comptroller
- Lieutenant Governor
- Attorney General
- Secretary of State
- Treasurer

Legislative Branch

General Assembly

- Senate (59 Members)
- House of Representatives (118 Members)

Judicial Branch

- Supreme Court (7 Judges)
- Appellate Court (52 Judges)
- Circuit Courts (865 Judges)

Local Government

Illinois has more units of local government than any other state.
It also has more cities, towns, and villages than any other state.
Most cities have a mayor-council form of government. For
example, Chicago has a mayor and city council. In Chicago, the
council makes most important decisions.

About two-thirds of the people in Illinois live in and around Chicago. Chicago often struggles with the rest of the state over money and power. The needs of Chicago, its suburbs, and the state's smaller cities and rural areas often conflict.

Key Issues

As Illinois continues to grow, its officials would like to decrease poverty rates. Between 1999 and 2001, the state

The Illinois state senate meets in this room to discuss and vote on social services, criminal punishment, and other important issues.

The Land of Lincoln

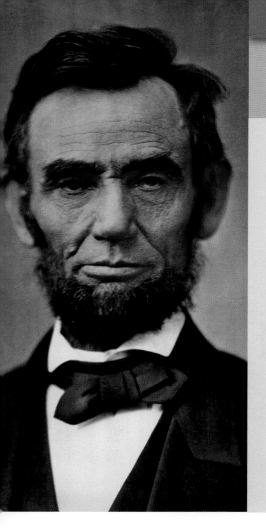

In 1834, Abraham Lincoln was elected to the Illinois state legislature. To study law, he sometimes walked 20 miles (32 kilometers) to get books.

Lincoln was elected president in 1860. As president, Lincoln guided the nation during the Civil War. He helped end slavery. But not everyone liked him. On April 14, 1865, he was shot and killed while watching a play at Ford's Theatre in Washington, D.C. His grave is in Springfield.

Illinois is proud of its ties to Abraham Lincoln. To honor the past president, Illinois calls itself the "Land of Lincoln." The General Assembly made this slogan the official state slogan in 1955.

increased social service spending by $1.3 billion. By 2001, the number of people receiving welfare dropped.

Illinois' government works to bring down the state's crime rate. In the 1990s, the state set up tough punishments for using a gun during a crime. It also gave law enforcement officers better equipment. In 1999, violent crime dropped 8 percent.

Soybeans and other crops provide a large part of Illinois' income.

Chapter 5

Economy and Resources

Like most states, Illinois has a mixed economy. Its position in the Midwest makes it a top agricultural state. But manufacturing, mining, and service industries also add to the state's wealth.

Agriculture

Fields of farmland stretch across Illinois. Farms cover about 80 percent of the state's total land area. The state grows more soybeans than any other state. Corn provides about 40 percent of the state's agricultural income. Illinois farmers also grow wheat, oats, fruits, and vegetables.

Farmers in Illinois also raise livestock. Illinois is among the top producers of hogs. Almost 10 percent of the farms in Illinois raise hogs. Illinois farmers also raise beef and dairy cows. Sheep and chickens are other common farm animals.

The number of farms in Illinois is decreasing, but farms are getting larger. Farms have more than doubled in size since 1959. Equipment makes it possible for fewer people to do more farm work.

Manufacturing

Farm machinery production raises billions of dollars for the state's economy. John Deere from Grand Detour, Illinois, invented the steel plow in 1837 to help farmers cut through tough prairie grass. Today, the John Deere plant in Moline still makes farm equipment.

Food processing adds even more money to the state's economy. Illinois has more than 950 food-manufacturing companies. Factories process the food grown by farmers. Meatpacking plants process Illinois' beef and pork. Other factories freeze and can vegetables. Quaker Oats and Sara Lee are based in Chicago.

Ray Kroc

In 1954, Ray Kroc heard about a restaurant called McDonald's in California. He visited the restaurant and made a deal to open others like it. He opened his first McDonald's in Des Plaines in 1955. Today, the chain, based in Oak Brook, Illinois, includes 30,000 restaurants in 121 countries.

Mining

Coal is plentiful under Illinois soil. The largest deposits are in southern Illinois. The state is sixth among the nation's coal producing states. Illinois workers mine more than 40 million tons (36 metric tons) of coal each year. The coal mining industry employs about 5,000 miners. Another 25,000 people work in jobs related to mining.

Illinois is ranked 14th among the states in oil production. Major pipelines carry crude oil and gas through the state. About 33,000 barrels of oil are produced each day.

Illinois also mines other minerals. Limestone, clay, and gravel are the main minerals found in Illinois. At one time,

Illinois was the nation's top producer of fluorite. Fluorite is used to make steel and aluminum. But fluorite mining ended in Illinois in 1995 due to high costs.

Service Industries

When Illinois' factories suffered during the 1970s and 1980s, service industries grew. Today, most workers in Illinois have jobs in the service industry. Rush-Presbyterian-St. Luke's

Medical Center in Chicago is one of the largest medical centers in the world. Real estate is another important service industry in Illinois.

Chicago is a center for financial institutions. The Chicago Stock Exchange, the Chicago Board of Trade, and the Chicago Mercantile Exchange have made finance a major industry in the state since the 1800s. Chicago also is home to large banks and credit companies.

Many Illinois workers trade grain and other products at the Chicago Board of Trade. They watch the screens to see if prices are going up or down.

Many people believe that rubbing the nose of this Abraham Lincoln statue in Springfield will bring good luck.

46

Chapter 6

People and Culture

Across Illinois, people honor Abraham Lincoln's place in American history. In New Salem, where Lincoln lived for six years, buildings have been restored. They now look much like they did when Lincoln lived there. In Springfield, people honor Lincoln's memory each February with a parade. People come from across Illinois and the rest of the country to learn about Lincoln.

Many events honor the immigrants who settled the state. Fulton celebrates its Dutch background with a parade and wooden shoe dance during Dutch Days. In September,

Did you know…?
In 1941, Wrigley Field almost became one of the first stadiums to add electric lights. Instead, the team's owner decided to give the equipment to the War Department to use during World War II. The field did not get lights until 1988.

Bishop Hill honors its Swedish culture with 19th-century harvest activities.

The roots of jazz and blues are in New Orleans, Louisiana, but Chicago also is known for this music style. Louis Armstrong, Benny Goodman, Miles Davis, and other musicians helped Chicago become a jazz and blues center. Festivals throughout the year feature jazz and blues musicians.

Sports

Sports fans across Illinois cheer for the pro teams in Chicago. Chicago has a football team, a basketball team, a hockey team, and two baseball teams.

Pro football has roots in Illinois. Formed in the 1920s, the Chicago Bears was one of the first teams in the NFL. George "Papa Bear" Halas coached the team to seven championships. One of his star players, Mike Ditka, coached the team to a Super Bowl win in 1986. In 1987, running back Walter Payton

Illinois' Ethnic Background

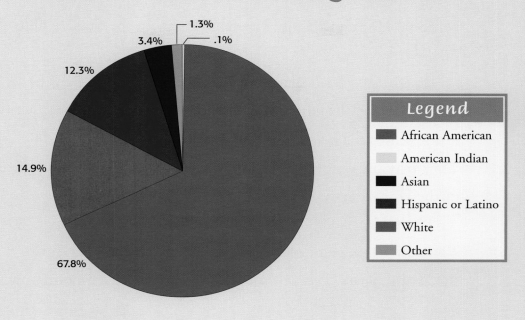

Legend
- African American
- American Indian
- Asian
- Hispanic or Latino
- White
- Other

1.3%
.1%
3.4%
12.3%
14.9%
67.8%

retired after 13 seasons with the Bears. He set many records during the years he played.

The Chicago Bulls struggled until 1984 when Michael Jordan joined the starting lineup. He began setting records. By 1991, the Bulls won their first NBA championship. In 1998, they won their sixth championship.

Hockey fans also can cheer for an Illinois team. The Chicago Blackhawks was one of the six original teams in the

National Hockey League. The team last won the Stanley Cup in 1961.

Baseball has been played in Chicago since 1871. Fans of the Chicago Cubs have cheered for the team through many losing seasons. The team last won the World Series in 1908. They play on Wrigley Field, the second oldest baseball field in the United States.

The Chicago White Sox last won the World Series in 1917. In 1919, eight players were accused of cheating during the World Series. People thought the players played poorly on

purpose in return for money from gamblers. The players were kicked out of baseball for the rest of their lives.

People of Illinois

Illinois continues to grow. Between 1990 and 2000, the population of Illinois jumped from sixth to fifth highest of all states. The population of Illinois increased by almost 9 percent. During that time, nearly every county grew.

Most of the people in Illinois are white. But their percentage is decreasing. In 1990, 78 percent of the people of

The Chicago Cubs baseball team plays at Wrigley Field in Chicago. Wrigley Field was the first stadium in the United States to use organ music.

Illinois were white. By 2000, that number had dropped to 68 percent.

African Americans make up an important part of Illinois. Few African Americans lived in Illinois before the Civil War. Many African Americans arrived between World War I and World War II to work in Illinois factories. Today, most African Americans in Illinois live in the Chicago area. More African Americans live in Chicago than white people do.

Today, Illinois is attracting people from Spanish-speaking areas and Asia. Many are moving to suburbs near Chicago and other cities. Naperville, near Chicago, has a large Asian population. Fairmont City has a growing number of Hispanic people. Across Illinois, people continue to arrive from India, Mexico, Korea, China, Pakistan, and other Asian countries.

Farmland and Skyscrapers

Because most of the people in Illinois live in or near Chicago, many people think of Chicago's tall buildings and busy streets when they think of Illinois. But tractors in the fields of rural Illinois are just as much a part of the state as Chicago's skyscrapers.

Large cities, small cities, farmland, and natural areas all make up Illinois. The differences make it an interesting place to live and to visit. The people of Illinois know their state is an important part of the past, present, and future of the United States.

The Starved Rock State Park in northern Illinois is known for its rich plant life and interesting rock formations.

Recipe: Frosty Apple

Illinois has many apple orchards. Golden Delicious and Jonathan apples are important fruit crops in Illinois. You can make this drink using apple cider.

Ingredients

6 scoops vanilla ice cream
1 quart (1 liter) apple cider
2 teaspoons (10 mL) nutmeg
6 scoops vanilla ice cream

Equipment

ice cream scoop
liquid measuring cup
blender
measuring spoons
spoon
6 large drinking glasses

What You Do

1. Let six scoops of vanilla ice cream soften at room temperature for about 15 minutes.

2. Put softened ice cream and 1 quart (1 liter) apple cider into a blender. Blend until well mixed.

3. With a mixing spoon, stir nutmeg into mixture.

4. Put one scoop of ice cream into each glass. Pour mixture over ice cream scoops.

Makes 6 servings

Illinois' Flag and Seal

Illinois' Flag

The Illinois state flag shows the Great Seal of Illinois on a white background. The word "Illinois" was added below the seal in 1969. It was added to make sure people know the flag stands for Illinois.

Illinois' State Seal

On the seal, an eagle sits on a boulder. The state motto, "State Sovereignty, National Union," is on the banner in the eagle's beak. A shield with 13 stars and stripes leans against the boulder. The stars and stripes stand for the 13 original states. A rising sun and a lake stand for progress. The date, Aug. 26th 1818, is the day the first Illinois constitution was signed.

Almanac

Nickname: Prairie State

Population: 12,419,293 (U.S. Census, 2000)
Population rank: 5th

Capital: Springfield

Largest cities: Chicago, Rockford, Aurora, Naperville, Peoria

Agriculture

Agricultural products: Corn, soybeans, wheat, sorghum, hay

Climate

Average winter temperature: 29 degrees Fahrenheit (minus 1.7 degrees Celsius)

Average summer temperature: 74 degrees Fahrenheit (23 degrees Celsius)

Average annual precipitation: 38 inches (97 centimeters)

Area: 57,918 square miles (150,008 square kilometers)
Size rank: 25th

Highest point: Charles Mound, 1,235 feet (376 meters) above sea level

Lowest point: Mississippi River, in Alexander County, 279 feet (85 meters) above sea level

Geography

violet

cardinal

Animal: White-tailed deer

Bird: Cardinal

Dance: Square dance

Fish: Bluegill

Flower: Violet

Fossil: Tully monster

Economy

Natural resources: Coal, petroleum, crushed stone, sand, gravel

Types of industry: Machinery, electronic products, printing and publishing, metals, food products, chemicals

Symbols

Mineral: Fluorite

Prairie grass: Big bluestem

Song: "Illinois," words by Charles H. Chamberlin and music by Archibald Johnston

Tree: White oak

Government

First governor: Shadrach Bond

Statehood: December 3, 1818 (21st state)

U.S. Representatives: 19

U.S. Senators: 2

U.S. electoral votes: 21

Counties: 102

Timeline

State History

1673
The Illinois Confederacy of American Indians lives in Illinois; Louis Jolliet and Father Jacques Marquette arrive in Illinois.

1763
Illinois comes under English control.

1778
Illinois becomes a county of Virginia.

1818
Illinois becomes the 21st state.

1871
Fire destroys much of Chicago.

U.S. History

1620
Pilgrims establish a colony in the New World.

1775–1783
American colonists and the British fight the Revolutionary War.

1861–1865
The Union and the Confederacy fight the Civil War.

1955
Ray Kroc opens his first McDonald's restaurant in Des Plaines, Illinois.

1968
The Democratic National Convention leads to protests in Chicago; more than 500 people are arrested.

1929
Al Capone's gang kills members of the Bugs Moran gang in the St. Valentine's Day Massacre.

1998
The Chicago Bulls win their sixth NBA championship.

1929–1939
The United States experiences the Great Depression.

1964
U.S. Congress passes the Civil Rights Act, which makes discrimination illegal.

1914–1918
World War I is fought; the United States enters the war in 1917.

2001
On September 11, terrorists attack the World Trade Center and the Pentagon.

1939–1945
World War II is fought; the United States enters the war in 1941.

Words to Know

agriculture (AG-ruh-kul-chur)—farming and ranching

colony (KOL-uh-nee)—an area of land settled and governed by a distant country

glacier (GLAY-shur)—a huge mass of slowly moving ice

habitat (HAB-uh-tat)—the place and natural conditions in which a plant or an animal lives

prairie (PRAIR-ee)—a large area of flat or rolling grassland with few or no trees

precipitation (pri-sip-i-TAY-shuhn)—the rain and snow an area receives

slogan (SLOH-guhn)—a phrase or sentence used by a group to express an important characteristic, a goal, or a belief

soybean (SOI-been)—a seed that grows in pods on bushy plants; soybeans are a good source of protein and oil.

territory (TER-uh-tor-ee)—a large area of land

To Learn More

Boekhoff, P. M., and Stuart A. Kallen. *Illinois.* Seeds of a Nation. San Diego: Kidhaven Press, 2002.

Donaldson-Forbes, Jeff. *Jacques Marquette and Louis Jolliet.* Famous Explorers. New York: PowerKids Press, 2002.

Heinrichs, Ann. *Illinois.* This Land Is Your Land. Minneapolis: Compass Point Books, 2002.

Oberle, Lora Polack. *Abraham Lincoln.* Let Freedom Ring. Mankato, Minn.: Bridgestone Books, 2002.

Internet Sites

Track down many sites about Illinois.
Visit the FACT HOUND at *http://www.facthound.com*

IT IS EASY! IT IS FUN!
1) Go to *http://www.facthound.com*
2) Type in: 0736815813
3) Click on "FETCH IT" and FACT HOUND will find several links hand-picked by our editors.

Relax and let our pal FACT HOUND do the research for you!

Places to Write and Visit

Governor of Illinois
207 Statehouse
Springfield, IL 62706

Illinois Department of Commerce and Community Affairs
620 East Adams
Springfield, IL 62701

Illinois Historic Preservation Agency
500 East Madison Street
Springfield, IL 62701

Lincoln Home National Historic Site
413 South Eighth Street
Springfield, IL 62701-1905

The Sears Tower, the tallest building in North America, stands 110 stories tall in downtown Chicago.

Index

T 57071

West Union School
23870 NW West Union Road
Hillsboro, Oregon 97124